LIKINGS FOR SHADOWS

BOOKS BY THOMAS TIMMINS

Novels
> *Blood Medicine*
> *The Special Fruit Company*
> *Down at the River*
> *The Hour Between One and Two (Trilogy)*
> *Aphrodisiac for an Angel*

Short Fiction
> *Puff of Time*
> *Visions of My Other Self*
> *Desert Dusk Music*

Graphic Verse Novel
> *Zom*

Poetry
> *I Was Just Laughing*
> *Likings for Shadows*
> *Buddhist Breathing in America*

LIKINGS FOR SHADOWS

Poems

THOMAS TIMMINS

ZOËTOWN MEDIA
HAYDENVILLE, MA

© 2016 Thomas Timmins
All rights reserved.

ISBN 978-0-9970287-5-1
Printed in the United States of America

Published by Zoëtown® Media
Zoëtown is a registered trademark of Zoëtown Media.
Haydenville, MA
www.thomastimmins.com

Book design by Maureen Moore, Booksmyth Press
www.thebooksmythpress.com

For everyone who believes in science

*"Today, near eventide, I did lead the girl
who has no seeing
a little way into the forest where
it was darkness and shadows were.
I led her toward a shadow that was coming our way.
It did touch her cheek with its velvety fingers.
And now she, too, does have likings for shadows."*

Opal Whiteley, age 4

from *The Diary of Opal Whiteley*.

Likings for Shadows

Questions,
Conjectures,
Facts,
Opinions,
Riddles,
Preposterous Declarations
Concerning
the Physical,
Biological, Emotional,
& Transcendental Natures
of the Most Unexamined
Fundamental Force
of the Universe

The force of attraction	*11*
Engima	*19*
Alchemy	*24*
Everyday hearts	*35*
Animals and things	*48*
Spirits	*61*
Artist's workshop	*69*
Random choices	*75*

The Force of Attraction

> *Seductive shadows*
> *swayed*
> *on the shade....*
>   Ken Kesey

The first shadow

When did the first shadow appear?
The instant God said
"Let there be Light!"

What if She'd said
"Let there be Shadow!"

Invitation

Softer than your lover's lips,
more supple
than the afternoon breeze
licking your ear,
the shadow of a cloud
loafs on the grass
inviting you to lie down
and remember who you were
before everything happened.

In the beginning

Light is the father of shadow.
Shadow is the mother of light.

Shameless

Erotic, promiscuous, shameless beings,
shadows touch and fondle everything,
penetrating and disappearing
into each other in full daylight,
reappearing and
falling into other shadows' arms
free as wind,
loose as rain.
Any time of day or night,
shadows crawl into strange beds
without a second thought.

Temptation

Shadow tempts light
while light seduces shadow.

Sparks

When lovers' shadows touch
before their bodies do,
shadows of sparks fly.
They strike the lovers' necks
like invisible cat whiskers.

Perfume

Ahhhh ...
the fragrant shadow
of a rose ....

Anchors

Without shadows to anchor them
to the earth, everything
and everybody would rise up
and float away.

Pas de deux

Firelight's favorite dance partner
is shadow.
They leap and twist,
jitterbug and waltz,
do the monkey and the box,
tango and merengue,
finally draping themselves over each other
slow dancing
until the fire exhausts itself
and flutters out in the arms of shadow
just before dawn.

Soothe

When it's
so bright
you can barely see,
your eyes crave
soothing in shadow.

Innocence

Without will,
without thought,
without feeling –
shadows are the only
truly innocent beings,
pure umbilical links
to the world
of instinct.

Dim

Hungry for the delicate rasp
of shadow on their eyelids,
soft paw of shadow on bare shoulders,
nick and scratch of shadow
on their thighs,
lovers leave the lights on dim.

Second story job

The treetop's shadow
slides up the house,
easing its way gently
over the bedroom windowsill
and steps silently down onto the floor.
The shadow arrives a little later today
but Emily D., holding a cupful
of poetry, waits
for it to arrive
for their daily tryst.

The future of love

With total selflessness
and complete attention,
shadows tempt,
caress,
enfold,
and merge
with humans,
plants,
animals,
rocks,
water,
wind.
light,
and dark.

Companionship

In loneliness
we prefer the company of shadows
rather than fellowship with light.
Like the song says,
"Me and my shadow
strolling down the avenue...."

Tide

At dawn. she lay on the beach
tangled in her thoughts
and exposed as a heap of driftwood shadows
inviting the tide to wash them away.

Tustle

Wrestling with tall peaks
heavy shadows sprawl
down the mountains' shoulders,
flopping over precipice
and fir plateau.

"Go on," the mountain groans,
"pin me. I'll give up."

Enigma

*To go in the dark with a light
is to know the light.
To know the dark, go dark.
Go without sight,
and find that the dark, too,
blooms and sings, and is traveled
by dark feet and dark wings.*
       Wendell Berry

Pass over

You can pass over
or move through a shadow
at the same time you
go under it.

Inside

To enter
a shadow,
you don't have to
slide, slip, or sneak.

You don't even have to try.

Jumping

Can you jump over your own shadow?

Scraps

Scraps of night
linger under the eaves,
between trees,
behind you,
shards of dreams
that left you breathless
with happiness
you can almost remember.

Doors

If shadows are doors to another world,
are they closed
or open?
If closed,
nobody needs a key.
If open,
anybody can blow right through
but never leave shadow behind.

Pounce

Just after sunrise,
still waking from dreams,
I drove the busy highway too fast.
A shadow of a bridge
pounced on my car.
I ducked and jerked
and veered into the next lane.
Cars honked and swerved
and squealed,
a herd scattered by shadow.

Sunlit, moonlit

Is the shadow behind
my sunlit body
the same as my
moonlit
incandescent lit
fluorescent lit
fireplace lit
candle lit
cloud lit
body?

Independence

Driving through heavy rain, I notice
in my smoky rear view mirror,
a car behind me
suddenly emerge into sight,
driving with lights out,
a smudge on the rain,
an autonomous shadow
having no visible source,
a shadow freed
now passing the car it hid behind.

Nocturnotropic

In sunlight, shadows following the day
array themselves around things
and, all day, grow away from the sun
like petals of flowers reaching out
seeking sustenance in the coming dark.

River

Like the river,
you can't step into
the same shadow
twice.

Day

A day without shadows
is a dark day
indeed.

The long patience of shadows

Coming or going,
present or absent,
you won't catch a shadow
watching the clock.

Plato

Our universe,
as we see it,
a well-lit cave
within the infinite mountain
of eternal shadow.

Alchemy

> *... the more light is cast upon a dark corner of a room, the more the other corners appear to be in darkness ...*
> Adolf Guggenbühl-Craig

Discovery

Discovery arises from shadow.
When an idea appears,
you say,
"It just dawned on me ..."

The evolution of pigment

Dark skin is due to
long exposure to sun
as pale skin is due to
long exposure
to shadow.

Resistance

Light is insistent,
shadow resistant.

Speed of light, speed of shadow

Flower shadows did not imprint
the concrete in Hiroshima
because the speed of light
is faster
than the speed of shadow.
The flowers disappeared
the instant before their shadows formed.

Weights

Using the most sensitive scale,
you'll find
a shadow weighs
less than light.

Measures

Impossible to measure precisely,
shadows confuse engineers.
The closer you come
to a shadow's edge,
the less defined it is.

The Engine

What if not the engine,
but the car's shadow
pulls it along the road?
That can't be right, you say.
What about driving in the country
on moonless, cloudy night?

Percentages

7% of all shadows that have ever existed on earth
have existed in the last 100 years.
26% of those exist today.
32% of all mobile shadows that have ever
wandered here
move through the world this very minute.

Math problem

If 4% of the universe is atoms,
and 23% of the universe is 'dark matter,'
and 73% of the universe is 'dark energy,'
how much of the universe is in shadow?

Iceberg

Why is a shadow like an iceberg?

a. It's a little chunk of a larger body.
b. It floats.
c. The further you trace it down, the bigger it becomes.
d. It might endure for a long time, but it's only temporary.
e. All of the above.

Flow

Like water,
shadows flow,
slowly sometimes
quickly at others.
They ooze,
leak,
brim,
and freeze,
but unlike water, they never
turn to slush
or crystallize.

Evaporation

When a shadow disappears,
it shrinks like ice
evaporating as it goes.

Organs

Do the body's
inner organs
have shadows?

Counting

How many shadows can one thing have?
Clue:
Think about the wooden statue of the Virgin
in Notre Dame Cathedral in Montreal,
or the Golden Buddha
in the Bangkok temple
both receiving prayers muttered at their feet
by thousands of swaying votive flames.

Basic physics

Shadow: energy or matter?
Neither.
Nor is it simply an
aspect of perception.
How do you prove it?
By answering the question
"Does shadow abide by
the law of conservation
of energy and matter?"

Absorb

When one shadow disappears into another,
which one absorbs the other?

Eruptions and archipelagos

Photos of deep space taken
from the Hubble telescope
reveal the universe
is an infinite sea of shadow
pocked with eruptions and
archipelagos of light.

Dimensions

A silhouette on a shade
has three dimensions –
one on this side,
one on the other side,
and one in between,
in the fabric.

Western world

Five elements compose the Western world:
earth,
air,
fire,
water,
shadow.

Eastern world

Six elements compose the Eastern world:
water,
wood,
fire,
earth,
metal,
shadow.

The logic of visible light

Visible light exists on a narrow band
of the electromagnetic spectrum.
Visible shadow exists on the same narrow band.

Thus invisible light
has its invisible shadow.

Combustion

Shadows don't burn.

Bullets

Fast film proves
what the human eye can't:
moving bullets have shadows.
What happens to the shadow
when a bullet penetrates
the flesh?

The dampness of shadows

When you rest under a tree
you can feel the shadow
moisten your eyelashes.

Surface

Rising from the sea floor
shadows dissolve the secrets of depth
in water's cold surface light.

Transparent

Clear glass itself
casts no shadows
unless it has bubbles
or scratches in it,
or a smudge
or fly squatting on it.

Modern cars and buildings
have adopted
high-tech smoked glass
so when you look out
you see the world
moving through shadow
and when you look in,
you wonder who's doing what
dark thing
inside the shadow.

Clues to the End of Time

Clues about the source of the Big Bang
and the ultimate End of Time
we learn from shadows:

1. Nothing is more like shadow than light.

2. Shadow will endure beyond time because
we have no mathematical law to describe shadow.

3. Shadows exist in all known and hypothetical
universes because they are integral to light.

4. If the stars burn out, or drop into infinite black holes,
the known universe will simply be a shadow of itself.

In the void, nowhere, nothing, not even shadow.

Everyday hearts

*The journal of the human heart for a single
day in ordinary circumstances.
The lights and shadows that flit across it;
its internal vicissitudes.*
Nathaniel Hawthorne

Secrets

Everyone has secrets
"... only the Shadow knows ..."

Vampires and ghosts

Most of all we fear
beings without shadows,
like vampires and ghosts,
and we mistrust "shady" people.

Hiroshima

How were human shadows
engraved in Hiroshima concrete
if not by the human desire
to use any means
to survive?

Lurking

Shadows simplify lurking.
Without shadows, thieves, spies, and kids
playing hide 'n seek
would be out of luck.

Mirror

In the mirror, under flat incandescence,
notice the depths in your wrinkles.
Intensify the light
or change the bulbs
to fluorescent tubes
and watched the brightness
wash away
the smudges
aging or sadness
dirty the flesh with.

Flashlight game

When the lights go out
do you play the scary flashlight game?
Holding the light under your chin,
welts and bruises rise from your skin,
darkness surrounds glinting eyes
revealing the monster
you've hidden under your face.

Thin

"My god, doesn't she eat?
She's thin
as a shadow...."

After naps

Human lights emerge
from afternoon shadows.

Hunting

In light,
when a shadow moves,
a hunter spots game
gambling.

Peter Pan

If Peter had not lost his shadow
when Nana slammed the window
as he fled,
and had Wendy not sewn it back on,
we would never have
come to love, hate, pity, and cheer
Captain Hook and the Crocodile.

My little girl

When I lean over to pick her up,
 where does my little girl's shadow go?

Does it rise into my shadow?
Docs her light displace
a part of my shadow?

Cosmic rules

In my voice
the shadow of night
which rules
the universe.

In my face,
the moon's dark side.
I see it
in your face, too.

Mammal babies

Most mammal babies
are born at night.

Clearcutting

Stop clearcutting forests.
The earth needs its tree shadows.
As they decline
we're all being forced
into politics.

History

The "long shadow of history"
is not a shadow,
it's a figure of speech,
unless you're referring to
Big Al History, the 6'10" accountant
standing on the beach
watching the sunset.

Wealth

No billionaire
can own a vaster treasure
of shadows
than the poorest child on earth.

Son's story

Where my pen meets the page,
it's as if the writing
emerges from the pen's shadow.
Does my life come out of the place
where my deepest memories
of my father's shadow
touches the blank page of my days?

Rich man

I know a rich man
who lights up his mansion
on the top of the hill with Klieg lights
every night, all night long, garden and deck,
driveway and pruned shrubs.
He protects himself and his family
from unknown threats
slinking in night's shadows.
To his friends he complains
about the high cost of electricity.
Have you met this guy, too?

Under the bed

When he was young,
he was afraid of the shadows
gathered in the corners of his room
and hiding under his bed.

"Now," he says, "the only shadow I fear
is the one in the corner
of the X-ray,
the one my doctor
can't stop squinting at."

Body magic

In the 1950s, American men worried
that the 5:00 shadow darkening their jaws
made them ugly.

Today, dark marks on their bodies, whiskers,
tattoos, scars, flaunt men's shadowy beauty.

A woman always uses shadow to power her sexual
beauty–eye shadow lusters the windows to her
soul; a love spot simmering on her upper lip tastes
of spice that nations have died for; in the shadowy
hollow of her throat, the promise of the pleasure
song.

Powerful lies

The lies of presidents and chiefs
bear shadows opaque and heavy
as mausoleum doors
built into humped earth.

Shadows and ghosts

Shadows and ghosts:
you can put your hand through both;
sometimes you can see both, sometimes neither, but you
know they're out there.

An old name for a wandering dead soul,
a ghost, is "shade." Look in the vast body
of the world's mystical, religious,
and fantasy stories, scriptures, and films
for evidence of sightings.

"Real" ghosts we've witnessed
make sounds, of course,
and poltergeist noises emerge from shadows with no known
source other than the mind of a twelve year old girl.

The King of Fools

Only the King of Fools
would send out his army
to conquer the flickering shadows
skulking
on the edges of the kingdom.

Democracy

In shadow,
ultimate democracy,
fraternity,
unity with all others,
no matter where
or who
or what.

Galaxy on earth

Satellite photos of the earth at night
reveal our primal campfire dreams
come true:
in our cities and towns,
we've become our own
galaxy of stars
afloat among mysterious deeps.

Mirage

A mile away, down the sunny runway,
a cargo plane emerges from the lake,
growing larger as it approaches.
Here, opposite the lake, in the plane's path,
a little boy stands with his father
watching and waiting.
As the plane rises,
the boy grips his father's hand tighter
and raises his other palm,
an umbrella over his head.
As the plane passes over,
the little boy feels its huge shadow
wash over him, soaking him instantly.
A second later, back in the sun,
his clothes and skin dry immediately.
He asks his dad what happened to the water.
When his father laughs
the boy doesn't understand,
but he looks up at the empty sky
and he feels like a silly duckling.

Foreshadowing

In the night room,
the shadow of your face
falls on mine,
closing my eyes,
opening my lips.

Animals and things

> *You can only come to the morning through the shadows.*
>
> JRR Tolkien

Blossoms

Shadow petals unfold
revealing the pistils and stamens
of things
to the eager swarms of light.

Crickets

Crickets perch partway up
the stems of grass
at the border between light and shadow
ringing vespers and matins
with tiny bells in their knees.

Fire, a quartet

Fuel,
heat,
oxygen,
flickering shadows.

Leaf

The shadowy underside of a leaf
grows as fast
as the sunny upper side.

Flowing

All day, the great shadows
flow west to east.
The little shadows dart here and there
like minnows in the river.

Baby shadows

At night, all the baby shadows
creep out of mama's warm and cozy bed
to play under the streetlights.
At sunrise, all the little shadows
slip back to their mother's breast.

Commanders of dreams

All night, great shadows pool
across the land.
The teenage shadows drowse
or sneak out of the house
to hang out mooning on street corners
or to flash through
the world's blue-lit living rooms
like scouts
sent out by the commanders of dreams
to get ready for their nightly skirmishes
in human brains.

Pillows

If shadows had pillows,
when they sleep,
they'd pull them over their heads
to keep out the light.

Smart mice

All mouse pups are born
familiar with the scent and the shape
of the cat.
The mouse pups who survive
notice early
and memorize
the dull shadow
of the crouching cat.

Ripple

Limp shadows ripple
across the soggy late afternoon.

Smoke

Smoke
floating off
cremated human flesh
casts no shadow.

Tree shadows

Cool, rainy days,
trees hug their shadows up
into their green bellies.
Longing to warm themselves,
they build shelters of shadows
over their boughs and branches.

Trucks

Rumbling down a sycamore-lined street
trucks pass through the showers
of shadow that pour out of the leaves
flowing over the trucks
spraying their metal bodies
then splashing with no sound,
puddling on the street.

Sky shadow

A photo of a C - 47 military cargo plane built to hold
a dozen tanks and trucks appeared on the front
page of the local newspaper.
A Greyhound bus hunched inside the fuzzy shadows
behind the mayor, the general, and the general's
staff. Later, I watched the plane trudge 1000' high
over town, avoiding enemy radar. Its shadow slid
over the ground, silent and harmless. Above, a dark
hole whined across the white sky.

An insect grounded

When I stroll downtown at night,
passing under streetlights,
my invisible twin's shadow shows up,
revealing himself to everyone
lingering on the evening stoops.

Waving my arms
I look down at my shadow.
Wings pump vainly
trying to raise my vast shadow body up
into the vague yellow light of the city night.

Gleamings

A shadow cast on pooled oil gleams,
as the shadow of a cormorant doused in crude
at sunset from a spill off the coast of Spain
gleams,
as the shadow of a young lover in a dusty
town rushing
to meet his girlfriend and seeing her
on the opposite side
of the newly oiled Main Street that looks as
wide as the Mississippi gleams.

Entropy Farm

My brother named his damp Oregon acreage
Entropy Farm.
The only things there that move
slower than decay
are banana slugs.
The only things that move slower
than slugs are their shadows.

A hobo's view

A constant flicker of shadows
crawls along under the train
as it climbs its ladder
of rails and ties.

Earth's palette

Shadows of clouds
that passed by years ago
lie under the surface
of eons of ice
compressed into glowing cobalt orbs.
In this age
when glaciers melt and recede
and the cobalt dims,
the earth's palette fades.

Doors

Shadows are the children of doors
closed to living room lights.

Pigs

Unlike pigs,
shadows lie in mud and slime
for hours without soiling themselves.
Shadows slide through blood and shit
in the slaughterhouse flood
without getting wet.
In fact, shadows guide warm blood
out of wounded bodies,
holding and shaping
the brilliant red pool
on the ground.

Cats, dogs, leopards, skunks, owls

If human eyes had the rods and cones
to see shadows that cats and dogs,
leopards and skunks and owls
can see,
would we have invented cities
or would we still be hunting
in the wild?

American flag in the breeze

Silky plume of green shadow
flutters over the shoulders
of a Mexican pepper tree
growing across the street
from the flag pole.

Giant

At dawn and sunset,
I stand on the hill, facing the sun.
Behind me, the shadow of my body
stretches for miles.

Repose

Country houses repose
in the shadows
of forests and hills.

Silhouettes

"Bright as broad daylight"
lightning silhouettes
oak leaves and cedar boughs
against a white night sky.

Snake

Desiring light and heat,
a garter snake slithers
among dry grass and shadows
all the colors of its scales.

All winged creatures

Starling shadows
flash across the pasture
like dark butterflies
flocking.

Waves

Never slipping,
the shadows of sails on water
mold themselves to the waves.

Margaret's oak

Her favorite tree
casts its shadow into the valley,
bowling over the shadow of the apple,

conquering any available light,
challenging the sun:

"More light!" the oak calls,
"more light!"

Wild roses

In the bright shadow of afternoon,
as I strolled along a wide arc of river,

the air grew dense
and fragrant around my body

as if I'd stumbled into
a rose garden gone wild.

Spirits

Shadows know the secrets of locked houses ...
Pablo Neruda

Breathless

When I stare at the dawning sun,
I feel breathless
as if drowning in darkness,
yet at sunset
my bones feel light
as a puff of wind.

Liminal

Waiting at the threshold,
between entry and exit,
between foreshadow and reflection,
I stand obscured
between worlds.

Non-violent tricksters

Shadows veil themselves
and distort day into night,
but shadows cannot wound,
and they can never
annihilate.

Divine

She first knew, with her whole
body, breath and mind,
herself as a divine being
when she saw the shadow of
Herself astride her horse
galloping in the sun.

Color

Most shadows come only in shades of gray
brown, and umber, but
observe the double rainbow.
The dimmer rainbow behind and outside
the original
is a rainbow shadow,
lustrous with all the colors
our eyes can see.

The god

The god of shadows
is the god of dreams.

Tears

In sudden desperation rising
on a Sunday afternoon
dry wind,
I topple onto the shade
and let myself weep
inside my shadow
sunk in grass.

Trust

Some people
don't trust
their own shadows.

Under my skin

Under my skin,
clinging to epithelium,
a thin shadow wraps my body
like a second, nerveless skin.
Before I sleep,
this shadow slips out through my eyes
into the night.
Before I wake up,
the shadow rides my breath back inside.

Evanescence

Like flames,
shadows
evanesce
in the wind.

Fearless

When light arrives
announcing itself
with a fanfare of colors,
silent shadow retreats,
but not far.

Natural law

Taoists,
Kabbalists,
Gnostics,
Calvinists,
Islamists
take note:
Study the humble shadow.
In it, you can find the truths
buried in all your teachings
cast by light.

The most useful shadow

The second most useful shadow
works the sundial.
What is the most useful?
The shadow you can hide in.

Getting to know you

If I mirror you,
I learn how you act.

If I shadow you,
I learn what you know.

Worship

In the sunlit nave,
adoration songs.
In the shadowed side altar,
whispered devotions.

Faith

Until we have
the technology
to weigh shadows,
we have to have faith
they are real
because we can't feel them,
taste them,
smell them,
hear them.
We can't even
intuit them.
It's true, we can see them,
but every judge and lawyer knows
the most unreliable witness is
the eyewitness–
three present at the same event
always see three different things.
Shadows exist
because we believe in them.

Between worlds

I slept deeply, on and on,
finally waking in a lightless place

where travelers stayed still
while new people and lands

came to meet them
before passing on

without leaving even a trace
of shadow.

Artist's workshop

Would that life were as abiding
as the shadow of a wall or a tree,
but it is as fugitive as the shadow
of a bird in flight.
An unknown Rabbi

Keen observers

Few people notice
shadows all around them
until someone points them out.

Natural colors

What color is the crow's shadow?
Name the color of apple blossom shadows.
What color flows off mountains
drenching roads, swamping farms, soaking cities?

Luminous

*For the kids at the California School
for the Blind and Deaf*

Living without light
is not a life lived in shadow.
We have other forms of illumination
and opacity
and we grow other senses
to know them.

"What about shadows in dreams?" I ask you.
"What do you mean, dreams?" you say,
throwing your unblinking eyes over my shoulder.

Writing

Writing:
the shadow
of speaking.

Artificial colors

On TV, red shadow signals
a rainy night city street,
blue the dusk under money,
yellow the tragic circus of accidents,
purple the reflection of age in a bar mirror,
green a golfer's reprieve,
white the horror of absence.

Words drunk on light

Lying on the paper
thirsty words on a page
toss back all the reading light
until they're soused.

Reader beware: If you tilt this page up,
the words' tipsy shadows might
slide off and leave you with
nothing but your imagination.

Grace

While some light is harsh,
sharp, jagged,
all shadows are graceful,
peaceful in harmony.

My gang

At night, I pass from streetlight
to streetlight
gaining shadows,
losing shadows,
some barely visible,
some hulking like giants,
some like fairy creatures sparkling
with distant light reflected in shards
of glass on the street.

Swaggering,
my gang of shadows crosses
the well-lit corner with me.

Time

Time began with the first sundial,
a peeled branch stuck in cleared dirt.
Before that, we lived in eternity.

View from inside

From inside a shadow,
you can feel your seeing.
On a sunny afternoon,
stand under a tree's leafy branches
and look out to the playing field.
Blue light reflects off green grass,
children's voices flow into your bower,
cool breeze streams past your face.
This is how, with shadow all around,
you learn to see with your every sense.

Photos

As difficult as they are to photograph
shadows are the only subjects
that make all photos, videos, and movies
possible.

Shadow plays

Shadow plays around the campfire
keep the kids laughing
and scare off the shadow creatures
watching from beyond
the fire's reach.

Random choices

I see my light come shining
From the west down to the east.
Bob Dylan

Shadow follows

Light drifts.
Shadow follows.

Light flows west.
Shadow flows east.

Light climbs up.
Shadow climbs down.

Light comes close.
Shadow withdraws.

Light retreats.
Shadow chases.

Light demands.
Shadow succumbs.

Light goes.
Shadow stays.

Resurrections

Night's vast lone shadow
wrecks on the sunrise
only to rise
fractured into an infinity
of companion shadows
for everything and everyone
exposed to daylight.

Longevity

Spotlights on a face
sponge off the shadows,
rejuvenating it,
eliminating depth,
reducing cheeks, chin, forehead, nose, lips
to flat up,
down,
a childlike now.

Experience

In the shadowy depth of my wrinkles
I see my history,
the singular tale of
my being.

Evolution

In the chaotic mess
of everyday's scrambles,
shadows go extinct
without a sound.

Reincarnation

When any shadow appears,
it's a brand new shadow,
sometimes resembling another,
as a child or a cousin
carries family traits,
but each shadow is unique.

Rest

Humans adore and crave light
but we go crazy
if we live in light alone.
We need to take our rest
under the shadow
of our closed eyelids,
practicing for
the longest nap of all.

Compassion

No shadow has ever refused
to sit quietly with anyone
of any race, color, creed,
in illness, health, or sorrow,
whether living, non-living, or dead.

Mercy

When I walk to town
on a hot July afternoon,
I creep from tree shadow
to merciful tree shadow.

Dream stage

The only shadow
in my dreams
is the carrying on
of nothing and everything else
blurred in offstage anxieties and
portentous flurries drizzling down
from the wings.

Your shadow

Do you have your light
the same way
you have your shadow?

Petrushka doll

In death, my corpse will be
a Petrushka doll of shadows:
on the outside,
my brain and blood darkened
under closed eyelids,
then my body shrouded in my casket,
then my life obscured in the grave,
then myself dimmed in others' memories,
then my soul gone with the forgetting,
then the final trace of my being
reduced to a gleaming chemical,
lingering in the chromosomes
of my children's children
and their cousins and their cousins,
and maybe, someday, your cousins, too.

Party time

When the party is almost over
and light says good night
because it has to get up early tomorrow,
shadows linger.

When the light disappears
and the host goes to bed,
shadows stick around.
They're just beginning
to have a good time.

Loss

Familiar shadows disappear,
like the shadows of a beloved tree cut
or great buildings fallen.
Light sobs in the new emptiness
until we raise a new tree or building,
as we must,
finding solace in the shadows reborn.

Secrets

Gravity whispers
through lips of shadow.

Painters know

Shadow limns the lit world,
giving depth and weight
to things.

Message from scavengers

Nine vultures soar gray sky
scouring the grass below
with eyes and noses gifted to match
unmoving shadows with
the first faint scent of meat's decay.

Shadowless

I walked late this March afternoon down a familiar back road. The sun shined like a distant reflection of itself in a cloud mirror sky so there were no shadows anywhere! I ground the mud under my shoes to compress it, to shadow it with more water, & tho the mud quivered, no shadow appeared. Nor did the melting snow beside trees bear shadow, nor the defiant lozenges of ice lying next to boulders darken with shadow. Imagining shadows, I saw that the snow still lying on the north sides of hills and trees was the symptom of shadows, the clue to where they have been and will return. A stream flowed and bubbled and a few birds called. Without shadows to ground my visual perception, the day felt eerie around me. Sound plodded, things seen stopped. My empty head drifted through a slaty light that covered everything in a soft woolly glow.

Silence

The silence of shadow
echoes
the silence of light.

Nothing

O,
it's nothing …
just
the shadow
of a thought …
a dream

passing …

Friends, rebel readers, writers in the storm, shadow watchers,

If you'd like to invite me to read from *Likings for Shadows* or from any of my other books, please contact me at tom@zoetown.com and I'll do my best to get there. I try to make my readings lively, interactive and, if the audience and I feel good chemistry, fun and inspiring. Please e-mail me your response to *Likings for Shadows* and I'll write you back.

Tom

www.ingramcontent.com/pod-product-compliance
Lightning Source LLC
Chambersburg PA
CBHW021135300426
44113CB00006B/437